WE'RE MAKING OUR HOME
A HAPPY PLACE

We're Making Our Home A Happy Place

Dale E. Galloway

TYNDALE
HOUSE PUBLISHERS, INC.
WHEATON, ILLINOIS

COVERDALE
HOUSE PUBLISHERS, LTD.
EASTBOURNE, ENGLAND

All Scripture quotations are from *The Living Bible* unless otherwise noted.

Library of Congress Catalog Card Number 76-8679. ISBN 0-8423-7860-X, paper. Copyright © 1976 by Tyndale House Publishers, Inc., Wheaton, Illinois. All rights reserved. First printing, October 1976. Printed in the United States of America.

I DEDICATE THIS BOOK
TO MY BEST FRIEND
AND WIFE, MARGI,
WHO MORE THAN ANY OTHER PERSON
IS HELPING ME TO BECOME
THE PERSON GOD CREATED
ME TO BE.

CONTENTS

Introduction

A marriage failure—yes, I have been there. A happy marriage—yes, my wife Margi and I with Christ's help are making our home a happy place. Believe me though, if it took being a perfect person to make a happy marriage you could count me out.

Out of the highs and lows of my own marriage experience I have come to understand that "a happy family is where imperfect persons are committed in love to other imperfect persons." Where each member of the family becomes an open channel of God's love to build loved ones' self-esteem.

A Christian family that is in step with God's perfect will becomes a mutual admiration society.

Never before in history has the family been under such devastating attack on all sides, yet in the midst of the conflict some are again discovering God's plan, principles, and promises for the making of a happy family. Those who already possess and practice the secrets of how to make home a haven of love and togetherness are the envy of millions. *Never has the candle of hope burned so brightly in the black of night as it does right now for all those who are determined to find a way to make their home a happy place.*

The fact that you have failed in the past doesn't mean you can't succeed in the future; it does mean you will have to try harder. If you have lost your first love, that doesn't mean you can't love again; it does mean you will have to love more. Facing insurmountable family problems doesn't mean you should give up and quit, but it does mean you should rise up and with God's help determine to climb a step at a time to the top. Having a good marriage doesn't mean you can't have an even better one, but it will take more effort on your part.

We're making our home a happy place—and so can you!

CHAPTER ONE
Be a Builder-upper

H. Norman Wright, in his book *Communication: Key to Your Marriage,* tells a vivid story about a sheepherder in Wyoming who, while observing the behavior of wild animals during the winter, saw a pack of wolves sweep into the valley and attack a band of wild horses. The horses formed a circle with their heads at the center and kicked out at the wolves, driving them away.

Then one day the watchful old sheepherder saw the wolves attack a band of wild jackasses. These animals also formed a circle, but they, unlike the horses, put their heads around the perimeter, placing their backsides in the center of the circle. When the wolves came, the jackasses started kicking like

13

everything, and they literally kicked the daylights out of each other.[1]

It seems to me that in every home we have a choice. We can be as wise as horses, and help each other, or we can be as stupid as jackasses, and kick each other to death.

The young man was the picture of success. At twenty-seven, he had already achieved more in the business world than most businessmen achieve in a lifetime. He told me about the manner in which he had showered his wife with expensive gifts, but she had literally thrown them back in his face. She wanted a hippie life, and she didn't want him or his materialistic friends. Taking his right hand and reaching as high as he could, while extending his left hand as far toward the ground as he could, he said, "This is how much self-confidence I used to have before I married her." Bringing his graphic illustration to the point, he put his two hands less than an inch apart and with strong emotion said, "This is how much self-confidence I have left after she has run me down day after day for the past three years." It is absolutely stupid to tear, claw, and gnaw at your mate. To be a tearer-downer is to be a destroyer of everything good.

1. Adapted from pp. 145, 146 of *Communication: Key to Your Marriage* (A Regal Book) H. Norman Wright by permission of Gospel Light Publications, Glendale, CA 91209. © Copyright 1974 by G/L Publications.

Today there are multitudes of people caught
up in the destructive game of tearing down
another person. Many TV entertainment
shows feature a sick humor that feeds itself on
tearing others down. First comes the slur, the
insult, and then the laugh. The truth is, this
kind of hurting one another isn't funny. It's
not funny on the tube, and it's certainly not
funny in the homes that are being torn apart by
disrespect for one another. Anyone can be a
tearer-downer. It takes: No brains, no
self-control, no learning from mistakes, no
God-power.

Most of us have been in a group when the
conversation gravitated onto an absent
person and soon the helpless victim was being
run down. Let's admit it. All of us have at some
time been caught up in these degrading
character assassinations. Be honest with
yourself: How do you feel inside when you
have stooped to the low level of running
another human being down? I know how I
have felt when I have fallen into this trap.
Either making or listening to negative
remarks about another person makes me feel
crummy. After indulging I feel that I need to
take a bath. What a downer! Jesus Christ has
come to lift us—to teach us not to be downers,
but lifter-uppers. For a more beautiful home
life, follow Jesus. Be a participator in his
mutual admiration society. "So encourage
each other to build each other up, just as you

are already doing" (1 Thessalonians 5:11).

To make your home a happier place in which to live, practice the biblical principle called edification. To edify means to build each other up. (See Romans 14:19.) Everyone agrees that in the majority of homes today, something is definitely missing. The biggest missing ingredient is the building up of each other in Christian love. There is nothing else that will add a touch of beauty to your home like your mastering the art of edification. There is no one who cannot, with Christ's help, become a builder-upper instead of a downer.

To make your home a happier place become a builder-upper.

EIGHT THINGS YOU CAN DO TO BUILD UP THOSE LIVING IN YOUR HOME:

1. *Shut the door on all verbal abuse.* Is there anything more degrading to a person than to be called derogatory names? On New Year's Day, along with 70 million other viewers, I watched the Rose Bowl game. Ohio State is my old home team, and for weeks I had looked forward to watching them play in their third straight Rose Bowl, and I did want to see them win. So I was greatly disappointed when they lost by one point. But what I hated more than the loss of the football game was when

TV cameras focused on head coach Woody
Hayes and flashed his profane name-calling
throughout America.

I can well understand the dirty-mouth
problem because I used to be one of the worst
offenders. My cleaning-up took place at fifteen
years of age when I invited Jesus Christ to
come into my heart and transform my life. He
changed the way I talked. If you don't know the
Lord Jesus Christ, this moment, let him come
inside your heart and clean you up so you can
speak words in your home that build up
instead of tear down.

What a pleasant difference it makes in the
family conversations when this verse is
observed: "Don't use bad language. Say only
what is good and helpful to those you are
talking to, and what will give them a
blessing" (Ephesians 4:29). For the best
results in all your communication, make it
your primary goal—to build up your mate.

Listen to yourself talk to your mate. Is your
conversation uplifting or downgrading? Are
you talking to him or her as a human being or
as a dog? Are you talking to your mate as you
want to be spoken to? "Little children, let us
stop just *saying* we love people; let us *really*
love them, and *show it* by our *actions*" (1 John
3:18). A great way to show it is to always
respect your mate's opinions and listen, even
when you disagree. Disagree? Yes.
Disrespect? No.

Refuse to blame or criticize your mate. Instead, restore ... encourage ... edify (Romans 14:13; Galatians 6:1). If someone verbally attacks, criticizes or blames you, do not respond in the same manner (Romans 12:17). "Be not overcome of evil, but overcome evil with good" (Romans 12:21, KJV). Not my way—but God's way. God's way is the winning way.

2. *Catch on to courtesy.* The number one rule for getting along with anyone is to treat him with courtesy. A certain minister made a habit of consistently asking one question of each partner before he would marry them: "John, I want you to promise me that you will always be as courteous to Mary as you are to other men's wives." Of course John nods, and says, "Yes, sir." He cannot imagine, at this stage of the game, anything else. Then the wise minister would ask, "Mary, will you promise that you will always be as courteous to John as you are to other women's husbands?" Unhesitatingly, Mary answers, "Yes." The point is—courtesy is not only a good preparation for marriage, but also a strong preservative of marriage.

Jane is twenty-eight and a beautiful single woman. John and his wife were talking with her the other day when Jane dropped something. Immediately John reached down and graciously picked it up for her. A moment later his wife dropped the baby's diaper bag, but John did not even attempt to pick it up, though it fell almost at his feet. Needless to say, Mary was hurt that he could be so thoughtless of her but so attentive to Jane. And she had every right to be hurt. It is shocking that men who have promised girls everything in order to marry them can then treat them with less courtesy than they would a completely strange woman. And who deserves our courtesy more than those we love most?

Courtesy costs so little and means so much that you can't afford to be without it. It may be some simple little thing, like opening the car door. A word of strong advice from the bold Apostle Peter to fellow husbands: "You husbands must be careful of your wives, being thoughtful of their needs and honoring them as the weaker sex. Remember that you and your wife are partners in receiving God's blessings, and if you don't treat her as you should, your prayers will not get ready answers" (1 Peter 3:7). Remember that "it is the little things we do or say that make or break the beauty of the average passing day." As an old nursery rhyme puts it:

> Hearts, like doors, will open with ease
> To very, very little keys,
> And don't forget that two of these
> Are, "I thank you," and "If you please."

"Love is ... never haughty or selfish or rude ..." (1 Corinthians 13:4, 5).

3. *Give each person who lives in your house that Golden Rule treatment.* What is the Golden Rule treatment? It is that treatment prescribed by Jesus to make home a happier place for everyone. Here it is:

"Treat others as you want others to treat you" (Luke 6:31).

Nothing you or I ever do can better express the life of Christ within us than to treat each individual as a person of worth and value.

Jesus never met an unimportant person.

It is all too easy to take advantage of those closest to us, to take out our frustrations on them, to take them for granted, to forget that they, too, have feelings. Father has feelings. Mother has feelings. Children have feelings. Everyone has feelings.

A marvelous opportunity is yours. You can make him feel like a king. You can make her feel like a queen if you put into practice this verse: "That is how husbands should treat their wives, loving them as part of themselves" (Ephesians 5:28). We can make that little boy feel like a prince, that little girl feel like a princess. Every time you are considerate of another person you show him that, to you, he is a person of worth and great value. For the greatest in family love—treat those close to you just as you wish to be treated: honored, respected, listened to, considered.

In a questionnaire, children were asked what they wished their parents would do and would not do. Three things stood at the top of the list:

1. "I would like for my father and my mother to welcome my friends and try to understand us."

2. "I would like for my father and mother to tell me what is right and wrong, but not to be too nasty about it."

3. "I would like for my father and mother to listen to me when I talk, like I'm a person who's worth something."

In each of these responses, the children are saying, "I want to be treated as a person of worth and of value."

Parents, treat your children as persons, and you will not have to worry about provoking your children to wrath. *The Living Bible* communicates the word of the Lord very clearly to us parents when it says, "And now a word to you parents. Don't keep on scolding and nagging your children, making them angry and resentful. Rather, bring them up with the loving discipline the Lord himself approves, with suggestions and godly advice" (Ephesians 6:4).

Children, the Bible says to you, "Honor your father and mother" (Ephesians 6:2).

To make your home a happy place, join Christ's happy mutual admiration society and treat other family members with kind consideration. As you treat your fellow family members with kindness, your home is going to be a happier place. The practice of mutual admiration is Christ's very best for the family unit.

4. *Establish bylaws on in-laws.* It was my privilege the other day to have lunch with an old friend. In the course of the conversation, my friend shared with me that for several months now, he and his wife have been separated. In the past several weeks he has made the discovery that both of them had been programmed by their own relatives to stay away from each other and encouraged to go ahead and get a divorce.

With moist eyes, my friend related that in a long overdue face-to-face conversation with his wife, they discovered that they still loved each other deeply. To be sure, the relatives were motivated by what they believed was best for their particular relative. I looked at my friend and said, "If you are going to make a success of your marriage, this is what you've got to do: Establish some bylaws on in-laws." Here they are:

1. Be loyal first of all to your mate. Do not allow any relative or anyone else to come between you. Your love and loyalty to each other is first and foremost.

2. From this day forward, neither of the marriage partners will make any negative remark about the other to any of the relatives.

3. Neither of you will listen to or allow any relative to make any negative comment about the mate that you have chosen to live with. If it happens, you will kindly ask them to stop, and refuse to listen.

4. Honor and respect your husband's or wife's relatives simply because you love your mate.

The Bible puts the solution to outside interference from in-laws in this nutshell: "If you love someone you will be loyal to him no matter what the cost. You will always believe in him, always expect the best of him, and always stand your ground in defending him" (1 Corinthians 13:7). Put this kind of love into action and it will wipe out your problem.

5. *Verbalize your appreciation again and again.* The desire to be appreciated is something we all have. It is amazing what one word of appreciation can do to kindle a new warmth in that other person's heart. Every family member should note that praise is the only paycheck mother gets for hours upon hours of work, day upon day, day after day. When was the last time you verbally expressed your appreciation to the woman of your home?

I wonder how many boys would like to carry papers every day of the year and never get a paycheck. I wonder how many teenage girls would like to babysit night after night and not receive any money for it. Or how many men would like to go to work day after day after day and not receive their overdue paycheck. It is about time we gave mother a paycheck: "Mother, thank you, I appreciate you for what you do in our home."

At New Hope Community Church where I pastor, we enjoy uplifting Sunday evening services, and one of the principles we practice in this service is the scriptural principle of edification (building one another up). Some thrilling things happen on Sunday nights. One night a young man stood to his feet and confessed that many times he had come short of God's plan and purpose in his life, but that God is faithful and God is teaching him. And then he turned around with a big smile and in a most beautiful way, expressed appreciation and thanksgiving to his wife. I tell you it was so great that I felt built up myself, and I can imagine how wonderful his wife must have felt.

Express your appreciation and you, too, will build your loved one up.

6. *Bring the best out of your mate.* He appeared uncertain of himself, and there were indications that he was drinking rather heavily. His wife, Lucille, phoned their

minister who went and bailed George out of jail. This was the start of a number of counseling sessions, during which Lucille spent most of the time berating George for his drinking, lack of purpose, and failure as a husband. The pastor listened to her criticize and complain for a long time in one session, then turned to George. "She told me ten thousand times that the whole trouble is me," George said. "She points her finger at me and begins every sentence with, 'the trouble with you is ...,' and I've listened to that phrase so many times that I'm sick of it."

A psychological test showed that in the area of self-reliance, Lucille had a score of 92, while George's score was 12. The pastor asked her if she felt that George was lacking in self-reliance when she had married him. "No," she said. "He was self-reliant and full of confidence. I don't know what's happened to him."

It doesn't take a pastor to see what had whittled down George through the years. To whittle down your own husband or wife is the most devastating thing you can do to your marriage partner.

It takes a wise woman to develop a man into a good husband. It takes a thinking man to bring the best out of his wife.

7. *Back up your mate in front of your children.* If you want children to run your home, then break this rule. If you want to

undercut your spouse and make him or her feel small and insignificant, then break this rule. But, on the other hand, if you want your children to live without confusion, if you want your husband to feel like a strong man, if you want your wife to feel like a secure woman—then back your mate up in everything she or he says to your children. Even if you do not agree with what is being said or with the discipline that is being measured out—that does not matter. Whether you agree or disagree at the time does not change the principle. Heed this penetrating word of truth spoken by Jesus: "Any kingdom filled with civil war is doomed; so is a house filled with argument and strife" (Luke 11:17). Stick together in front of the children or hang separately—you choose.

8. *Remember this: Love overlooks a multitude of faults.* I have faults. If you lived in our home, you would know some of my faults. We all have our faults. Every man, every woman, every boy, every girl has good points and other points. "Be humble and gentle. Be patient with each other, making allowance for each other's faults because of your love" (Ephesians 4:2). Center on the other person's faults and you are going to be miserable, and you are going to make that other person miserable. Center on the positive, and the positive will increase.

The other day I heard a poignant story that

will haunt me for a long time. A young mother
left her small child unattended while she was
doing the laundry in the basement. The child
found some adult medicine, drank it all, and
was dead on arrival at the hospital. The mother
sat, stunned and stricken, waiting for her
husband to come. What would he say? He
idolized the child. When he did come, he took
his wife in his arms and said just four words,
over and over: "Darling, I love you." Nothing
else, no questions, no incriminations, no
blame. Just: "Darling, I love you." He forgot
about his own hurt and did his best to draw the
protective cloak of his love around his
suffering wife. That man had learned to
really love.

*I love you for better, for worse, for richer, for
poorer, in sickness, and in health.*

Yes, Lord, I want to be a builder-upper of
those I love and not a tearer-downer. Thank
you, Jesus, for showing me your more excellent
way.

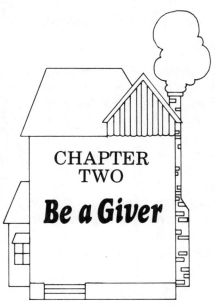

CHAPTER TWO

Be a Giver

A Christian friend who has a good marriage relationship shared with me that a few years ago his marriage had become stale. It seemed that the fun, the joy, and the excitement was not there. He said, "We came to the point where we discovered what the problem was. We had fallen into the rut of taking instead of giving. When we started giving, our marriage came alive again." Jesus said in effect, You want to enjoy life more abundant? Then you've got to give yourself. "For if you give, you will get! Your gift will return to you in full and overflowing measure, pressed down, shaken together to make room for more, and running over. Whatever measure you use to give—large or small—will be used to measure what is given back to you" (Luke 6:38).

The number one destroyer of homes today is selfishness. Many marriages are in trouble because people refuse to give to each other. It takes only one person in a home saying, "I want what I want when I want it," to disrupt the entire household. Being a selfish taker comes naturally. It is the way of the natural man apart from God. Heed the Word of God when it says, "Don't just think about your own affairs, but be interested in others, too, and in what they are doing" (Philippians 2:4). What a difference there is between a selfish taker and a generous giver.

A *taker* demands a lot but hardly ever gives.
A *giver* always gives and does not make many demands on other people.

A *taker* is a perpetual griper.
A *giver* is always thankful and grateful for what he receives.

A *taker* says, "I want you to please me."
A *giver* asks, "How can I please you?"

A *taker* thinks only of his own needs and wants.
A *giver* considers the other person's needs and desires.

A *taker* tries to change his mate.
A *giver* wants to change and improve himself.

A *taker* says, "It's you against me."
A *giver* says, "We will stand together in this situation."

A *taker* does not stand by his spouse in discipline of the children.
A *giver* stands by his spouse in discipline of the children.

A *taker* sees the worst in his mate.
A *giver* sees the best in the loved one.

A *taker* tears his mate down.
A *giver* builds his mate up.

A question for you—which kind of person do you think would be the most fun to live with, a giver or a taker? A better question yet, which kind of person are you? Are you a selfish taker or are you a generous giver? Which one do you want to be? Let's be honest and admit there is the child of rebellion within all of us. Good news: We don't have to live a selfish life—Jesus has come to transform us, to change us from takers into givers. "Therefore if any man be in Christ, he is a new creature: old things are passed away; behold, all things are become new" (2 Corinthians 5:17, KJV).

THE MORE YOU GIVE, THE MORE YOU GET.

Most of the problems people have in marriages stem from a lack of giving first. I often say,

"Show me a marriage that's falling apart and I'll show you two people who are trying to get from each other instead of giving first."

Learning to give first stopped a cold war in the Brown home. "Our marriage wasn't exactly on the rocks," Dennis said. "It was more like a cold war. The warmth and affection had gone out of our relationship." Dennis and his wife, Kathy, were like two strangers living in the same home, not smiling, not touching, hardly ever talking to one another. Dennis said, "I wanted Kathy to show me affection first." Kathy said, "I wanted Dennis to first give to me, then I would give back to him." So it went on, a miserable cold war.

Then one Sunday, the Browns came and listened to my sermon. And in God's perfect timing, that summer day I was talking about "How to Have a Happy Home." During the sermon I said, "I know there are people here today who have fallen out of love, who at one time were much in love. But I tell you today that if you will give first, I believe you can fall back in love."

Unknown to me at the time, God took those words and used them to speak to the Browns in their cold war. Later relating what happened next, Dennis said, "That morning, you asked everyone to join hands with the person they were with and pray with you. We squirmed uncomfortably. Kathy sort of glanced at me and I glanced back. Actually, we felt embarrassed. But we decided to put our feelings aside and try it.

"From that morning we started praying together, our whole relationship began to change. It was only in a small way at first. When I'd come home in the evenings, Kathy would have the house shining and be in the kitchen humming softly as she prepared the evening meal. She would greet me with a smile and a kiss, and I found myself giving in return, being more thoughtful, helping with the children and the house. And one day we realized that we were in love again. The change started when we let God teach us to give first."

It's impossible to give anything away.

This story is told about an old country preacher. He stood by an open grave, performing the last rites for a member of his parish. It was winter. The icy wind pitilessly penetrated even the warmest garments. The preacher was shivering and heroically trying to keep his teeth from chattering during the committal service and the final prayer. He had no overcoat on—a pathetic contrast to the heavily clad folk who were gathered about the grave. The woman who wrote about it said, "I knew what had happened without asking. He had given his overcoat to someone else. He was that kind of a man."

What kind of person are you? What kind of husband are you? What kind of wife are you? What kind of teenager are you? What kind of boy? What kind of girl? Are you the giving kind? Or are you the withholding, the taking kind?

Try giving yourself away.

Your family needs what you have to give. Your wife needs what you have to give her. Your husband needs what you have to give. Your parents need what you have to give. You are the only father your daughter has. You are the only child just like you that your mother has. Each family member has something to give that other family members need. How foolish and how selfish to withhold what you can give to those you love. Give what you can give: give your friendship, interest, thoughtfulness, understanding, appreciation, empathy, time.

The more you give the more everyone in your home gets.

Sometimes we only think we are giving. When we allow God to show us the way, we discover that we are being selfish, wanting the other person to be the one to change. Here is a letter from a lady who, for a long time, thought her husband was the one who had to change:

> Then one day God opened my mind and let me see all the mistakes I had made—the many times I had failed to give my husband the assurance of my love that he so desperately needed. My inner vision was buried under tons of self-pity. I was saying in effect, "If you don't love me, I won't love you." I was expecting to receive his love and attention without first giving to him.
>
> I was a good Christian (or so I thought). I took the children to church regularly but I just "walked out around" my husband. My life was completely separated from him. Actually, I suppose I was wrapped in a cloak of self-righteousness. But I soon realized that he could find no place for himself in my life and, even worse, our children were following the example.
>
> Thank God for the lesson, "Be the first to give"—I have seen the light. Asked for God's forgiveness. The change is taking place. I'm not asking for my husband's love, just assuring him of mine by giving lovingly to him. When I do something for him or smile and say something nice, it's like seeing a small part of glory when his eyes light up.

The seeds of discontent are in the expectation. More times than not, marital dissatisfaction is the result of secretly demanding that one's mate, by some extrasensory perception, perceive all our emotional needs and promptly meet them. How unfair it is to expect someone to know something we have not told him. You can save yourself untold frustration if you will accept the truth that no one person can satisfy all of another person's needs. Each of us is a many-faceted person, and to expect some other person to match each mood, satisfy each demand, and fulfill each need, is simply unrealistic. Worse yet, it is selfish. Save yourself a lot of discontent and obey this timely advice: "Don't be selfish; don't live to make a good impression on others. Be humble, thinking of others as better than yourself" (Philippians 2:3).

Center all your attention on your own needs and you will find yourself disillusioned and disappointed every time. Jesus gave us the number one clue to marital bliss when he said, "Give, and it shall be given to you" (Luke 7:38, KJV). It is when one learns to first discover and meet the needs of his spouse that something beautiful called love happens. What greater way to show your love than to unselfishly respond to your mate in doing your best to meet her need.

To go on a delightful adventure tonight,

why don't you take your loved one in your arms and ask this simple caring question, "Honey, what are your needs? What can I do to make you happy? What can I do to make our relationship more satisfying?" You do this and your marriage is going to come alive with new fulfillment and understanding. If you want to experience the miracle of closeness in your marriage, then be the first to give and keep on giving.

How can our partners know we're loving or in love if we don't act like it? Or if we don't say it from time to time? Marriage can get exciting when love is expressed. When was the last time you said to your mate, "I love you"?

As I work with married couples, a common complaint of wives is, "He doesn't kiss me any more." When I try to find out the cause, almost always I get the same answer: "When we were first married, he wanted to kiss me while I was washing the dishes, and I told him to let me alone until I finished."

Frances Hunter, in her book on marriage, responds to this happening with these words: "Girls, let me tell you, I'm never too busy to stop whatever I'm doing to kiss my husband. Often I am in the finishing stages of dinner when he gets home. When he comes into the kitchen he always asks what he can do to help. Do you know what my standard answer is? I just say, 'Kiss me on the back of the neck—that's all!' And that's what he does!

And never is it a source of irritation or something that slows down my getting supper. If it slows down getting supper—Praise the Lord! Our love is far more special than food any day.

"If women would just learn to make their man feel like a man, it is amazing what would happen to their marriages. If they prized the kisses of their husband, it's amazing how many more they would get. When a woman lets her man *know* he's a man, he'll do anything in the world for her."[1]

Men, your wife wants to be shown by word and action that you love her. If you love her, tell her so. Want a more exciting marriage? Then *never stop courting and finding ways to express your love.*

John, the disciple, who with the maturing of years abounded with love, said it this way: "Dear friends, let us practice loving each other, for love comes from God and those who are loving and kind show that they are the children of God, and that they are getting to know him better" (1 John 4:7).

There are a thousand exciting ways to express your love:

Wives, show your love by meeting your husband at the door looking your best. Watch him hurry home next time.

---

1. Charles and Frances Hunter, *How to Make Your Marriage Exciting* (Glendale, California: Regal Books, 1973), p. 21.

There is nothing more effective than a
welcome listening ear to make your
mate feel close to you.

A phone call to say you will be late tells your
wife you are considerate of her.

An unexpected card or note saying: "You
are special to me, I love you."

A little thing like opening the car door, or
carrying something heavy for your wife.
Let her know she is your queen. Keep it
up and don't be surprised if she begins to
think you are her king.

One evening when I had to be away from
home I stopped at a phone booth and phoned
Margi, my wife. I said, "I called to tell you I
love you, and I think you are the neatest." I
noticed that several days later she was still
talking about this. Then a few days later
Margi surprised me by going and buying me
some clothes she thought I needed. I liked the
clothes, but better yet, I felt loved. You want
your marriage to be exciting? Then never,
never stop expressing your love.

Christ's kind of love will carry you through
almost every storm of life. And the only way
that this kind of love can come in and stay in
your heart is for the Spirit of Christ to come
into your life. Somehow the self-centered
backbone in our spirit has to be broken. This is
what Christians mean by "conversion" or
being "born again." Christ comes in and
changes the basic attitude. The most important

thing in any marriage is having Jesus Christ. How our homes need Christ's saving love that is ... "never haughty or selfish or rude. Love does not demand its own way. It is not irritable or touchy. It does not hold grudges and will hardly ever notice when others do it wrong" (1 Corinthians 13:5). What a love Jesus gives!

LET JESUS MAKE A HAPPY GIVER OUT OF YOU.

Trouble in homes is not new; it is as old as man. Jesus told a story about a young man who was having conflicts with his parents. The big problem was that he wanted what he wanted—he was one immature selfish sinner. His attitude was evidenced by his words to his brokenhearted father, "Give me." He took his father for every cent he could and left home.

The prodigal son journeyed to a far country away from parents' rule. He discovered that sex, removed from God's will, is empty, disappointing, and ugly. Someone has said, "Self-gratification is ever a one-way street—with a hogpen at the end."

As the young man remembered that his father's house always had "bread enough and to spare," he discovered that the "horrible religious inhibitions" were not as bad as he had once thought. He began to sense that there is a close relationship between proper inhibitions and abundant blessings.

When he returned, repenting, and the father received him with open arms, the son said, "Make me a servant." In the father's arms another selfish taker was transformed into a generous giver.

Yes, it is giving that fills a home with joy, while selfish taking is the destroyer of harmony in homes. Perhaps the most important question of this book is, "How do I become a generous giver instead of a selfish taker?" There is only one place to start and that is in establishing a personal relationship with Jesus Christ. You can never have God's best until you give him your best. God loves you so much. He wants to come into your life and help you have an exciting and happy marriage.

CHAPTER THREE

Be a Peace-maker

Do you know what a beef stew marriage is? It is a marriage in which the husband is always beefing and the wife is always stewing. Unfortunately, there are a lot of homes in which trouble is brewing.

Eloise said, "Dad, Mom and I were sitting at the breakfast table when we started discussing my future plans. Somehow I said the wrong thing. I said my life as a married woman would have very little outside activity, that I wanted to be a homemaker. Immediately, my mother reacted and said that I was blaming her for working outside of the home. I really didn't mean to cause a fight, but I sure did! She told me I was ungrateful, unwilling to help around the house. I reacted and said some terrible things that I shouldn't have said. I love mother very much, but why is it we always have such a difficult time getting along together?" Let's admit it—it isn't always easy to get along with those you love.

Nowhere in the world is there more fighting and trouble than in many homes. The oldest battle of all is the battle in the home. The longest war that was ever fought was not in Viet Nam, but the one that goes on, and on, and on, inside the family: fighting, conflict, quarreling, cutting one another. Needed: Peacemakers to make home a happier place. What a contrast between a peacemaker and a selfish troublemaker.

A *peacemaker* responds to people.
A *troublemaker* reacts.

A *peacemaker* forgives.
A *troublemaker* holds grudges and is set on evening the score.

A *peacemaker* sees not only his side of the story, but tries to see the other side.
A *troublemaker* sees only one side ... his side.

A *peacemaker* gives room for the other person to be right and for himself to be in the wrong.
A *troublemaker* always says, "I am right and you are wrong."

A *peacemaker* leaves things in the past
where they belong.
A *troublemaker* drags out the past and uses it
as an axe to chop with when he is losing
the argument.

A *peacemaker* controls his anger with
Christ's help.
A *troublemaker* often loses his temper and
vents his anger on others.

At home with your family, which kind of
person are you? *A peacemaker?* or *a
troublemaker?*

One mother said to me, "I'm so tired of the
bickering and the quarreling and the fighting
in our home, I could walk off and never come
back."

Feeling empathy, I said to this dear lady, "I
understand how you feel. It must be very
disturbing to live in all the conflict." I
continued, "You long to have peace and
harmony in your home, is that right?"

She said, "I'd give anything to have a more
peaceful and happy home." Giving the troubled
mother a warm smile to soften the blow, I put
this penetrating question to her, "Tell me,
are you a part of the problem or are you a part
of the solution? Are you a happy peacemaker or
are you a disturbing troublemaker ... which
are you?"

While she was still dazed by my

straightforward question, I explained, "God is concerned about the conflict and fighting in your home. The Bible tells us that God is the God of peace. I am convinced upon the authority of the Bible that he wants to give you peace. The fact is that while we were yet troublemakers, fighting against God, that he sent his Son, Jesus Christ, to make peace with us. As the Scripture explicitly announces to us: 'Christ himself is our way of peace ... making us all one family, breaking down the wall of contempt that used to separate us' (Ephesians 2:14). The truth is that before we can be at peace with other people, we must make our peace with God."

After she had admitted that she had been more of a troublemaker than a peacemaker, I had the joy of telling her that if she would invite Jesus Christ to come into her life and be her Lord, he would change her from being a selfish troublemaker into a real peacemaker. "There is therefore now no condemnation to them which are in Christ Jesus, who walk not after the flesh, but after the Spirit" (Romans 8:1, KJV). Our world is full of people who are at war with others simply because they are not yet at peace with God.

As this lady opened her heart and prayed a prayer of commitment to Jesus Christ, the miracle of Christian conversion took place, and her very nature was changed and she became a new person in Christ Jesus. As long as I live I shall never forget the beautiful serenity that I saw in her eyes when she said, "Pastor, I think my home is going to be a happier place now, thanks to Jesus."

Here is your answer for a more peaceful home—let the Prince of Peace, Jesus, come into the center of your life. This very moment, surrender yourself to Jesus Christ. Let him change you from being a selfish troublemaker into being a peacemaker. It was Jesus who pointed to the true mark of his followers when he said, "Blessed are the peacemakers: for they shall be called the children of God" (Matthew 5:9, KJV). A true Christian is not perfect in his life of peacemaking, but he possesses an enormous desire to make peace with everyone.

I especially like this description of a Christian given by the Apostle Paul in Ephesians: "Now your attitude and thoughts must be constantly changing for the better. Yes, you must be a new and different person, holy and good. Clothe yourself with this new nature" (Ephesians 4:23-24).

With Jesus as your Lord you, too, can be a maker of peace.

LEARN HOW TO HAVE MORE PEACEFUL DISCUSSIONS

Drop that piece of glass. What a horrible sight to see a man, a wife, and their children with pieces of glass in their hands, lashing out at each other, slicing each other to pieces. Somebody do something! Stop it! It's murder! Yet this is exactly what members of a family do to each other emotionally when they allow themselves to be driven into a sequence of reactions intended to hurt one another.

As most of us live together with our families from day to day, we are going to experience differences of viewpoint. Life wouldn't be any fun if we all thought alike. Any normal family is going to have arguments, fights, debates, discussions, or whatever you choose to call them. The peacemaker's goal is not to eliminate all discussion in the home, but to make sure that the discussions are Christian ones rather than brutal, harmful, cutting battles that leave persons wounded and bleeding.

Quarreling is what you don't need. *The Living Bible* says: "It is hard to stop a quarrel once it starts, so don't let it begin" (Proverbs 17:14). Discussions you must have for the benefit of mutual understanding.

To avoid quarreling and yet benefit from peaceful, creative discussions in your home, follow these important ground rules.

1. No name-calling. Absolutely *no* name-calling.
2. Control your temper. If your emotions begin to heat up, then cool it; stop the

exchange until you have cooled down
and can think straight. "A fool is
quick-tempered; a wise man stays cool
when insulted" (Proverbs 12:16).

*Things can only get out of hand if you
allow yourself to get out of control.*

*When the emotion heats up, the mind
stops working.*

3. Do not criticize the other person. "Most
    important of all, continue to show deep
    love for each other, for love makes up
    for many of your faults" (1 Peter 4:8).
4. Do not make accusations. "Stop being
    mean, badtempered and angry.
    Quarreling, harsh words, and dislike of
    others should have no place in your
    lives" (Ephesians 4:31).
5. Do not be sarcastic. It creates a bad
    atmosphere in a discussion and will
    soon cause it to degenerate into a hurting
    fight.
6. Do not be argumentative. "In
    everything you do, stay away from
    complaining and arguing" (Philippians
    2:14).
7. Leave the past in the past. Don't pick
    up that past and use it as an axe to chop
    with when you are losing the argument.
    "Love forgets mistakes; nagging about

them parts the best of friends"
(Proverbs 17:9).

8. Do not jump to conclusions. "Any story
sounds true until someone tells the
other side and sets the record straight"
(Proverbs 18:17).

9. Listen to the other person's viewpoint.

10. Keep the discussion on the issue and
refuse to attack the person.

11. Do not try to prove who is right and who
is wrong.

12. Never forget what the Bible says, "A
soft answer turneth away wrath: but
grievous words stir up anger" (Proverbs
15:1, KJV).

13. Develop a sense of humor. Seeing the
funny side of things and laughing at our
own mistakes helps tremendously to
keep us relaxed. I agree with the
preacher who said, "If you could just sit
on the fence and watch yourself pass by,
you would die laughing at the sight."

*A peacemaker is one who learns how to
disagree agreeably.*

A Christian life is one of growth, change, and
continuing to become more like Jesus. As a
follower of Jesus, put off the old way of
meanness, bad temper, quarreling, harsh
words, and being hard to live with. Put on

Christ's way; be kind to each other; be tenderhearted; forgive one another. (See Ephesians 4:23-32.) And "try always to be led along together by the Holy Spirit, and so be at peace with one another" (Ephesians 4:3).

STOP TRYING TO CHANGE THE OTHER PERSON—LOVE HIM.

A young couple who came to me seeking help had a common problem. In their struggle to change one another they had become very irritated with each other. It seems one liked to sit up and watch the late show, and then sleep late the next morning. The other liked to go to bed early and get up at the crack of dawn. They wanted me to tell them who was right and who was wrong. I took the opportunity to explain to them that no two people are alike and that this problem was just a basic difference in their makeup. One was a night person and the other was a day person. They could save themselves a lot of heartbreak if they would simply accept the difference in the other person, and allow that person to be his or her own self. In conclusion I said to them, "Try to change your mate, and you are in for a civil war. Accept your mate for the person he or she is, and you have taken a giant step toward harmony."

Some years ago, the late Casey Stengel and his wife were being interviewed on national television. At the time Casey Stengel was one of America's most famous baseball managers. It was their golden wedding anniversary and Casey was celebrating it as you might expect—by managing a baseball game. Mrs. Stengel remarked, with a twinkle in her eye, that at one time she had tried to instill a love of fine arts into her husband. "I took him to Rome and Florence," she said, "and tried to get him to go to the art galleries, but all he wanted to do was stay in the hotel and talk baseball to the bellboys."

Of course he did; he was being himself—the great baseball manager. And this lady had the good sense to finally allow her husband to be himself. By the way they looked at each other, everyone could tell that here was a couple who loved more and more every year of their marriage.

People naturally resist change. Do we resist suggestions for change when they come from our mate? We rebel every time. I do. You do. Save yourself a lot of frustration and bring a new sense of freedom and relaxation to your marriage by practicing this universal law of mind and spirit:

> *I can change no other person by direct action. I can change only myself. When I change, others tend to change in response to me.*

Change yourself before trying to change others. In the greatest sermon ever preached, Jesus, explaining how to have beautiful attitudes and right relationships, said: "Don't criticize, and then you won't be criticized. For others will treat you as you treat them. And why worry about a speck in the eye of a brother when you have a board in your own? Should you say, 'Friend, let me help you get that speck out of your eye,' when you can't even see because of the board in your own? Hypocrite! First get rid of the board. Then you can see to help your brother" (Matthew 7:1-5).

Keith Miller, in his book *The Taste of New Wine,* in a chapter entitled "Christian Marriage," tells about his conversion and the two years he was a Christian and his wife wasn't. He so desperately wanted to share his newfound joy and wonderful life in Christ with his wife, Mary Ellen. He tried every way he could think of to convince her that she should do the same thing that he had done—commit her life to Jesus Christ. It seems perfectly logical that a husband who has been deeply committed to a living Christ should set about trying to get his wife converted. But the harder Keith Miller tried to convert his wife, the more cold and upset she became. Later, she told him that all she could hear him say was that they had been happily married for five years and suddenly he didn't like her as she

was, that he wasn't going to accept her fully
unless she changed into some kind of
religious fanatic.

Keith Miller said, "Finally, I realized the
unchristian pressure my trying to force Mary
Ellen into my version of a Christian wife,
was having in her life. We were drifting apart.
Although things looked happy on the surface,
we both knew that our marriage was bruised
and broken on the inside where the world
could not see. Finally, one night I said to her,
'Honey, I can't deny the tremendous things
which have happened to me these past two
years, because of trying to give my future to
the finding of God's will, but I have been
wrong in trying to force all this on you. No one
forced it on me. I'm sorry I tried (however
unconsciously) to manipulate you by taking
you to all these meetings, etc., to get you
converted. I am really sorry.' I went on to tell
her, 'When we got married I didn't sign up to
change you, just to love you ... and I do, just
as you are.' "

You talk about relieving the pressure valve.
As a result of Keith's open confession and
change in attitude, all that pressure that had
been building up was gone, and there was
relaxation and freedom once again in the Miller
home. Within a few weeks Mary Ellen went
out and made a beginning commitment of her
future to Christ all by herself in a way which

was right for her.[1]

As peacemakers, it is not our job to change the other person. It is our job to love them. Husbands, it is not your calling to change her; it is your calling to love her. Wives, it is not your job to change him; it is your job to love him. When you get right down to it, you can't change anyone. It is God who does the changing. Let God change your mate and you are going to make your home a happier place.

You are called by God to be his peacemaker in the midst of conflict.

When there is conflict between ourselves and someone else, the human tendency is to start pointing out who is right and who is wrong. Give it to 'em, man! Show 'em what's what! Does trying to prove who is right and who is wrong ever bring people together in understanding? It never has yet. It only compounds the bad feelings and makes more and more trouble.

To be a peacemaker in the midst of conflict, do these four things:

1. Expose and confess to God the real cause of your own wrong attitude. "If we confess our sins, he is faithful and just to forgive us our sins, and to cleanse us from all

1. Adapted from *The Taste of New Wine* by Keith Miller (Waco, Texas: Word Books, 1965), pp. 46, 47. Used by permission of Word Books, Publisher, Waco, Texas.

unrighteousness" (1 John 1:9, KJV). *God, I confess to you my anger caused by a selfish attitude. Thank you for forgiving me.*

Whatever the other person has done or not done, I am responsible to God for my own attitudes and actions.

2. Acknowledge your own inadequacy. *God, I can't change this wrong attitude by myself; only by the power of the Holy Spirit working within me will it change. Thank you for changing me even now.*

3. If your wrong attitude has been brought out by what someone else did to you, forgive the other person. Do as the Bible tells you to: "Be kind to each other, tenderhearted, forgiving one another, just as God has forgiven you because you belong to Christ" (Ephesians 4:32). The sooner you forgive, the more Christlike you are becoming. So "be gentle and ready to forgive; never hold grudges. Remember, the Lord forgave you, so you must forgive them" (Colossians 3:13).

A lady came to me for counseling. It came out that she harbored a long-standing resentment against her husband. He had been unfaithful to her. "I can forgive him for anything else, but not for that," she said, and there was a finality about her declaration. I suspected a direct relationship between her burning hostility and her physical disability. I asked her if she would prefer the continued suffering to forgiving her husband. She said, "I will *never* forgive him!"

Then I said, "I think it would be fruitless for me to pray for you, since you have not met one of the basic conditions for answered prayer. Jesus makes it clear that you cannot be forgiven (healed spiritually, emotionally and physically) until you are willing to forgive anyone who has injured you." Listen to what Jesus said: "Your heavenly Father will forgive you if you forgive those who sin against you; but if *you* refuse to forgive *them, he* will not forgive *you*" (Matthew 6:14-15). The woman departed, grim and unyielding. I had no definite assurance, of course, that her physical pain bore a direct relationship to her unforgiving nature, but the edict of the Bible on this matter and the findings of modern science point to a definite correlation. The mind simply passes its pain and disease on to the body.

For the best of personal and family health, be the first to forgive.

4. If you have done something wrong to a member of your household, ask him or her to forgive you. Your responsibility is not what the other person said or did but

your own bad behavior. It is so easy to con oneself by saying, "He did that to me, so I can do this to him." Don't deceive yourself. "Lies will get any man into trouble, but honesty is its own defense" (Proverbs 12:13).

If *you* have done wrong, then you need to confess to your loved one and ask for forgiveness. For healthier and happier family relationships, follow this restoring principle: "Confess your faults one to another, and pray one for another, that ye may be healed" (James 5:16, KJV).

Fred is late again for dinner and Norma is furious because her carefully prepared meal is ruined. Throughout the meal they sit in silence. Fred feels guilty, but his pride won't let him say, "I'm sorry." Instead he goes to the kitchen with Norma and helps her with the dishes or puts up the hooks in the closet, a job she has been asking him to attend to for weeks. Or if he has to go out again that evening, he comes home with candy or flowers. All these are substitutes for the honest apology he needs to make.

Suppose during dinner, Fred admitted his fault and said, "I'm sorry, dear. I could have phoned and should have when I knew I was going to be late. Will you forgive me?" Then Norma would have likely responded, "There was no need for me to be nasty. Will you forgive me?" Relief comes, then a smile and a kiss and the renewed warmth of fellowship. There is no substitute for the asking and the giving of forgiveness.

Without forgiveness, no human relationship can continue. No home can continue. No friendship can exist. No church can continue. Without forgiveness, no business, no school, no activity can be sustained very long.

Forgiveness is the key to enduring love. The more forgiveness, the more love.

> *To activate healing medicine, speak these three words: "I am sorry."*

For the best results when asking for forgiveness, follow these rules:

1. The sooner you ask for forgiveness, the better.
2. Confess no one's sins but your own.
3. After stating what you have done wrong, admitting you are sorry, ask, "Will you forgive me, please?"

A middle-aged father has been a bear to live with all week, causing trouble in the entire family. Finally, toward the end of the week, during his prayer time, he comes to realize that he is the family problem. He admits to himself and God that he has been disturbing the peace because he feels his right to have sex with his wife has been denied. Immediately he confesses his selfishness to

God and proceeds to ask each member of the family to forgive him for his selfish behavior and bad attitude. The results are beautiful—harmony in the home.

Question: When you are wrong, do you make it a practice to verbally acknowledge this to members of your family?

With God's help, be the first to ask for and the first to give forgiveness. Do this and you are going to make your home a happier place to live!

> *"Blessed are the peacemakers, for they shall be called the children of God"* (Matt. 5:9, KJV).

CHAPTER FOUR
Be a Communicator

Every fall at our church we sponsor an Institute for Successful Marriage. These five-week classes are made up of men and women of all ages who have the common desire of wanting to make home a happy place. In the open discussion that we have at the Institute we have confirmed what many marriage counselors have been saying: The foremost problem in the home is the problem of communication.

Every marriage that breaks down,
breaks down first in communication.

It's not by accident that some couples are happier than others. What is it that causes one couple to be happy and another to be unhappy? It is not that the one couple has fewer problems than the other. The happy couple has learned to share, to communicate one with the other; the other couple has not learned the joy of sharing openly together.

Communication is the core of a happy marriage.

A young couple preparing for matrimony came in to see me not too long ago. I said to this young couple, "Remember this: every marriage has problems because we are people and people have problems. Those who persistently converse one with another together hammer out solutions to marriage problems. If you will communicate with each other, you can find solutions to every marriage problem that comes your way."

Essential to a happy marriage is the determination to converse, openly and freely, in a spirit of love.

A committed Christian has the inside track to making his home a happy place. As we yield our lives to Jesus Christ, we yield right of way to his spirit of love to work in us and through us. What joy it is to have Jesus Christ leading us in this all-important area of talking and listening.

**TO MAKE YOUR HOME A HAPPIER
PLACE, APPLY THESE FOUR
PRINCIPLES OF COMMUNICATION:**

1. Listen more—talk less. Most of us talk too
much and listen too little. James said it
loudly and clearly: "Dear brothers, don't ever
forget that it is best to listen much, speak
little, and not become angry" (James 1:19).

Communication is a two-way street. It
involves both talking and listening. I wonder
why it is so much easier to talk than it is to
listen. It seems that listening should come
naturally, but it doesn't; it requires effort.

How well do you listen to the members of
your household? When your mate is talking,
or when one of the children is trying to tell
you something, how well do you listen? Do you
know how to listen—or do your eyes stray and
betray your disinterest? Do you find yourself
thinking about what you are going to say
next—or do you listen to what the person is
saying now?

Being a poor listener is a bad habit. But I
have good news for you. If you are not a very
good listener, and that takes in an awful lot of
us, you can break the habit. You can change.
Jesus said, "If any man has ears to hear, let
him hear" (Mark 4:23, KJV). Start right now
to put forth the effort to intentionally
concentrate on what the other person is saying.

One teenager said, "My friends listen to what

I say, but my parents only hear me talk. How can I tell my father my problems? He brings work home every evening. Dad is not the type who sits and listens. He sits and tells you how it is. We rarely discuss anything important at home. We used to talk at dinner, but now that is out. Dad bought a portable TV and put it in the dining room. I can't ask my mother any questions about sex, because right away she fires back, 'What do you want to know for?' "

Don't let this be true of your son or daughter. Instead, "Share each other's troubles and problems, and so obey our Lord's command" (Galatians 6:2).

Eric Hoffer tells about a peasant woman who cared for him after his mother died and during the years that he was blind. "This woman, this Martha, took care of me. She was a big woman with a small head; and this woman, this Martha, must have really loved me, because those eight years of my blindness are in my mind as a happy time. I remember a lot of talk and laughter. I must have talked a great deal, because Martha used to say again and again, 'You remember, you said this; you remember, you said that . . . ?' She remembered everything I said, and all my life I've had the feeling that what I think and what I say are worth remembering. She gave me that. . . ."

You, parents, can do a great deal to enhance and to build your child's self-esteem. How? By intentionally listening when he talks to you. "When others are happy, be happy with them. If they are sad, share their sorrow" (Romans 12:15).

A lesson that love has been teaching me in recent days is, love says, "Look at the person you are talking to. Go ahead, look at him. Don't look up there at the ceiling. Don't look over there. Don't put your hands in your pockets or draw on the ground. Don't kick the tire, just look at him."

Not long ago I was sitting in our living room, reading, when my wife, Margi, called, "Dale, Dale . . ." After several tries without response, Margi said, "You don't listen when I'm talking to you." I said to myself, "I'm not that kind of person; I'm warm, friendly, caring, outgoing . . . (I preach that to people all the time). After all, haven't I been listening to people all day? Now I want to read my book."

Love says: "I'll put the paper down. I'll turn the knob off. I will look. I will listen. And all of me is present here to listen to and to look at you."[1]

Isn't that what love means? All of me is here—at attention, to care, and to will your good. Family members are dying for someone

1. Adapted from *We Really Do Need Each Other* by Reuben Welch (Nashville, Tennessee: Impact Books, 1974), pp. 98-100.

who will listen, who will care, who will look, who will understand and hear. With Christ's help, we can change our homes if we will love this way.

A young man sitting in my office was expressing with great pain what he was feeling. If only he could get his wife to talk. I have heard this expressed repeatedly by lonely family members longing to share with another person they love or care about.

Why don't people talk? Here are some of the reasons that I have heard some people give:

1. Because you don't give me a chance.
2. Because you don't really listen.
3. Because you come through as not really caring what I say, what I feel.
4. Because you would become defensive.
5. Because I am afraid you will think less of me.
6. Because you make me feel so stupid.
7. Because I just don't trust you that much.
8. Because you act like you know all the answers.
9. Because you always have to be right.
10. Because I'm afraid you won't accept me as I am.

Seek first to understand, not to be understood. Have you ever said: "He doesn't understand me"; "She doesn't understand me." I can tell you from personal experience that as long as a man is exclusively preoccupied with being understood by his wife, he will be overrun with self-pity and trapped in his own miserable self. I have a sneaking idea that women sometimes become just as self-centered and consequently make themselves just as miserable.

One of the smartest prayers you can pray is this: "Lord, grant that I may seek more to understand than to be understood . . ."

What a superior way God gives us to live in his Word: "You should be like one big happy family, full of sympathy toward each other, loving one another with tender hearts and humble minds. Don't repay evil for evil. Don't snap back at those who say unkind things about you. Instead, pray for God's help for them, for we are to be kind to others, and God will bless us for it" (1 Peter 3:8-9).

Wonderful communication happens when a husband or a wife becomes lost in, engrossed in, understanding the other person. Learning what makes the other one tick, what the other one likes, dislikes, feels and needs. (See Ephesians 4:2; Philippians 2:2-4.) Those who seek first to understand become the communicators of love. You do want to communicate his love—don't you?

What greater way to love—than to listen?
What greater way to say, "I care about
    you"—than to listen?
What greater way to help the other person
    feel important—than to listen?

What greater way to learn—than to listen?
What greater way to understand your
    mate—than to listen?
What greater way to earn the right to be
    heard—than to listen?
Make the Psalmist's prayer your prayer,
"Create in me, O God, a listening heart."

*If you really listen to your mate, he or she
will then listen to you. It's fun—try it!*

2. *Don't allow trivial things to break
down your communication with other
members of your family.* In the play,
Philadelphia, Here I Come, a success in Britain
and on Broadway, one sees the pathetic and
heartbreaking attempt of a father and son to
break through the silence and habits of years.
On the eve of the son's departure from Ireland
for America, neither father nor son can sleep.
Late at night they go to the kitchen for a
snack and are surprised to meet each other
there. They search for words, but can't find
them; they plunge into painful silences.
Nonverbal communication to the audience
indicates how hard they are trying to get the
barriers down and communicate during these
last hours together before their final
separation.

And then, as if he were inspired, the father
begins to talk about when the son was ten
years of age and they went fishing together.

Through sharing the recollection of this happy memory the long standing barriers begin to drop and at long last father and son are enjoying communication with one another.

The boy said, "You know, that was one of the best times of my life, Dad. I'll never forget that little red boat, and the good times we had together fishing."

"No," contradicts the father, " 'twas not a red boat; 'twas a blue one." The son said, "It was a red boat!" "No," said the father, "it was a blue boat!" And the argument is on.

Tragedy ensues as each contends for his memory of the insignificant detail to be accepted as correct. Stubbornness on both sides brings back the separation and alienation and the curtain falls on the spectacle of two lonely people, unwilling to remove the barriers that isolate them from each other.

What trivial things often separate family members: edgemanship, wanting to be right, and clinging selfishly to one's position. How tragic that we allow such little things to become barriers between us and stop communication. All because we have to be so proud, so stubborn, so right. Suppose you do win the argument. But if you have created a gulf and each person is alone and lonely, everyone loses. The way always to win is never to allow the trivial to create gulfs in your family. Make togetherness your aim—and whatever you do, don't allow trivial things to erect barriers between you and your loved ones.

Exercise tongue control. In the book of James in the New Testament, the tongue is compared to the rudder of a ship; although the rudder is a small part of the ship, it turns the ship in any direction and determines its destiny. What husbands and wives say to each other can either help or hinder, heal or scar, build up or tear down.[2]

Don't settle for anything less than complete control of your own tongue. Only a fool rattles off anything that comes into his mind. (See Proverbs 29:20.) 1 Peter 3:10 says it like it is: "If you want a happy, good life, keep control of your tongue, and guard your lips. . . ." Controlling your own tongue is not easy to accomplish in your own strength. You can do this only with the Spirit of Christ living in full control within you. Let God have his complete way with you.

Don't nag. Nagging is constantly harping or hassling your mate for one reason or another. A technical definition is critical faulting, but whatever it is called, it irritates and frustrates marriage partners—the "nagger" as well as the "naggee." Solomon said in the Old Testament, "A nagging wife

2. H. Norman Wright, *Communication,* p. 60.

annoys like a constant dripping" (Proverbs 19:13).[3]

One woman asked, "What can I do when after many months he still hasn't fixed the door?" Simply ask him if he wants to do it this week or if you should hire someone to do it. Make up your mind that for once you are not going to turn into an old nag, because you have more horse sense than that!

3. *Never stop expressing yourself–just learn to do it better.* Prolonged silence is not golden; it is a cruel weapon. Phyllis McGinley penned these words: "Words can sting like anything, but silence breaks the heart." When communication is broken off, things are at their worst. I have known husbands and wives who would go for days without speaking to each other. At the breakfast table the father would say, "Johnny, tell your mother to pass the bacon." They wouldn't talk to one another day after day after day. That is horrible. It's destructive. It hurts. How it hurts every member of the family. Whatever you do, don't stop talking to each other.

The Bible gives us some great advice. It tells us to settle our differences on the same day they arrive. "Let not the sun go down upon your wrath" (Ephesians 4:26, KJV). Keep talking and listening until you work out your

3. H. Norman Wright, *Communication,* p. 173.

differences and arrive at a mutual point of understanding.

Say what you mean. One of the key problems in communicating is making yourself understood. Sometimes we think we have said it, when we haven't. What you meant to say, what you actually said, and what the other person heard are often three very different things. This illustrates why it often takes extra effort to clearly communicate your exact meaning to others. The old proverb, "Say what you mean and mean what you say," is a most worthy goal. So let's work at it.

Question to ask: "Am I saying what I really mean?" A wife criticizes her husband as he sits at the dinner table hidden behind his newspaper. She says, "I wish you wouldn't slurp your coffee." What she means is, "I feel hurt when you hide in the newspaper instead of talking to me." Be straightforward; learn to say it like it is, gently if necessary, but clearly. The Bible says, "There is a right time for everything . . . a time to be quiet; a time to speak up . . ." (Ecclesiastes 3:1, 7).

Learn to speak the truth in love.

On a Sunday afternoon as I finished teaching the first class session of the Christian Life and Witnessing Course for the upcoming Billy Graham film, I had an uncomfortable experience. A man I had never seen before

introduced himself, warmly shook my hand
and said, "Thank you for the uplifting
session. I have heard a lot of speakers, and
your spirit was really of Christ. But if you will
allow me to speak the truth in love, I thought
the one illustration you used about the old
man shooting his wife distracted from the
truth you were wanting to get across." My new
acquaintance smiled in Christian love, I
thanked him, and he went out the door.

I admit I felt defensive at first. Who is that
strange man anyway? Does he have his nerve!
But I couldn't forget the warm handshake, the
smile, the Christian love he had
communicated. My next level of thought was,
"Well, that's only his opinion. I think it is a
good story, and besides, it is fun to tell."

The following day as I was preparing to
repeat the same lesson to the Monday night
class, I took another look at my material. Do
you know what I discovered? My friend was
right; now I was thankful he had told me.

Epilogue—Weeks later at our big city-wide
film crusade, after I had finished giving the
audience an invitation to come to the front
and make a personal commitment to Jesus
Christ, who should I see but my new friend.
There he was, a counselor, leading someone to
Jesus. I waited until he was free, walked over
to him, and said, "It's good to see you, friend."
He smiled and said, "The Spirit really spoke
through your voice tonight in a beautiful way."

I believed him and it made me feel good,
because I knew he was one who spoke the
truth in love.

The deepest relationships are built on the
unbeatable combination of truth and love.
Anyone who builds a relationship of any kind
on less than openness and honesty is building
on quicksand. Such a relationship will never
stand the test of time, and neither party to the
relationship will draw from it any noticeable
benefits. The Bible tells us in Ephesians 4:15,
"Let us speak the truth in love: so we will fully
grow up in Christ" (NEB).[4] As we do, the
results will be meaningful interpersonal
relationships one with another.

Jesus' way to handle daily irritations in the
family is by *"truthing it in love."* Sometimes
we hold a husband or wife accountable for
our feelings, but they know nothing about
them. How unfair this is for everyone. For the
good of all, when something is bothering you,
speak up and speak the truth in love. Handle
your irritations daily and you will avoid the
big emotional blowups.

We are all tempted to think that
communication of an unfavorable emotional
reaction will tend to make waves. If I want to
tell you that something you do bothers me, I
may be tempted to believe that it would be
better not to mention it. Our relationship

4. *The New English Bible,* Oxford University Press, 1961.

will be more peaceful; you wouldn't understand anyway. So I keep it inside myself. Each time you do your thing, my stomach keeps score: two ... three ... four ... five ... six ... seven ... eight .... One day you do the same thing that you have always done and all hell breaks loose. All the while you were annoying me, I was keeping it inside and somewhere, secretly, learning to hate you. When the explosion came, you didn't understand—and I was surprised myself. And it all started when I said, "I don't like what she's doing, but it would be better not to say anything. The relationship will be more peaceful." What I did was not avoid trouble—but save up dynamite for the big explosion.

To speak the truth in love is to learn to report honestly and openly your own ideas and feelings. "This is the way I feel." "This is my viewpoint." "I don't know why this bothers me, but it does." Don't blame the other person or make him to be all wrong, and yourself all right.

No one has the right to be another's judge—that's playing God. Who but God can read the intentions and motives of another? "Judge not, that ye be not judged," Jesus said (Matthew 7:1, KJV). Leave the judging to God.

Say it with love.

The best way to express yourself, either verbally or nonverbally, is with the love of Jesus. Dr. Robert Schuller, of the renowned Garden Grove Community Church in California, was recently traveling on a plane from the West Coast to Chicago. Sitting in the first class section on the plane, Dr. Schuller noticed to his right a woman who had a close-fitting bandana on her head. He just glanced at her and then went on working; little did he realize that this woman was a very famous person.

As the airplane was approaching O'Hare Airport in Chicago, it became apparent that traffic was so heavily backed up that day that they wouldn't be able to land for approximately thirty minutes. The pilot came on the intercom and said, "Folks, we'll be flying around here for about thirty minutes before we can land, so just relax and go ahead and have another cup of coffee on us." This statement hit the woman in the bandana as being hilariously funny, because, if you have ever traveled in the first class section of an airplane, you know the passengers don't drink coffee—they drink a lot of something else. At the captain's coffee suggestion this lady let go with the big laugh, and instantly the people who heard her laugh exclaimed in one accord, "Phyllis Diller!" and she laughed all the more. Everyone enjoyed a good laugh together. Phyllis Diller's laugh had given her away. Dr. Schuller said that as he got off the plane that day, he couldn't help but ask himself, "As a Christian, does my love give me away, that I am a Christian?"

Let Jesus put love into all of your verbal and nonverbal communication. To make your home a happier place, express yourself in the spirit of Christ's love.

4. *For the greatest in family communication, together converse with God.* How sad it is that all too many homes are depriving themselves of the tremendous joy that Jesus wants them to have simply because they neglect praying together. It is sharing with God through family prayer that opens the door to greater sharing between members of a household.

> *Hearts open to God invariably open to each other.*

Charles Jones, a well-known salesman, shares this:

> I imagine this is hard to believe, but I lectured all across America on confidence and courage to thousands of people while I couldn't get up enough courage to pray with my wife and family. It took three years. I was afraid they'd be embarrassed or think that I was getting too religious. But I knew it was my responsibility to

lead the family, and something needed to be done to bring us closer together. I never knew my wife or children well until finally I began to use a little courage to express love and leadership through praying together.

One of the great blessings in my life came one night when my wife and I prayed together. I don't mean we made religious noises; we just talked to God about some things we couldn't seem to say to each other.

I remember I was irritated with her over some little things, and that's why it hit me so hard. She prayed first that night and said something like this: "Dear God, thank you for this good husband you've given me, forgive me for not being a better wife, help me be better."

As she prayed, her words crushed me. I could see very clearly she wasn't at fault. I was the scoundrel. I wasn't the husband I should have been. I wasn't the father I could have been. What a great lesson ... the only way I could begin to learn it was on my knees. If she had said those things to my face I would have suspected her of trying a new approach to get her own way.[5]

5. Charles Jones, *Life Is Tremendous* (Wheaton, Illinois: Tyndale House Publishers, 1968), p. 72.

My wife and I enjoy doing many things together, but one of our very special moments is when we pray together. There was a time when I didn't think prayer was all that exciting.

Many times prayer strips away the veneer of our lives and in our honesty to God we become more honest with each other. As we draw close, so close to God, we draw close, so close to each other. It is in prayer that we are made one in the Spirit.

Many couples kneel or sit when they pray. We have also done that, but some of our best prayer times have been lying in bed with our arms around each other. As we lie there in each other's arms and pray, there is a closeness, warmth, nearness, oneness together with our Heavenly Father. This kind of intimacy cannot be accomplished in any other way. At that moment we are one with God and all is well in our world. What enormous strength comes from these close prayer times together.

If you can't pray together, then pray for your mate in private. Many of you are the only Christians in your home. Pray for your mate. Let God love that other person through you. What beautiful communication God's love is.

As your family prays together, you will not only experience a new inner feeling of togetherness, you will communicate more effectively with each other. Prayer is the best way to get the barriers down. When a family openly prays together, their ideas blend, their wants blend, their needs are openly shared, and they truly become one in the bond of love. "But when the Holy Spirit controls our lives He will produce this kind of fruit in us: love, joy, peace, patience, kindness, goodness, faithfulness, gentleness, and self-control" (Galatians 5:22-23).

Above all else, "always keep on praying" (1 Thessalonians 5:17), for it is in prayer that a family learns to speak the same language of love.

CHAPTER
FIVE

Be Fun to Live With

What about it? Are you fun to live with? Do you think the people in your home enjoy your company? Or do you find yourself being more like a wet blanket that dampens the spirit of fun in your family?

In a recent issue of Dr. Norman Vincent Peale's newsletter, *Foundation for Christian Living,* he quotes from an article in *Reader's Digest* where Bob Hope writes about the place of fun, laughter and happiness in human experience. Hope tells of an incident in 1948 when General Dwight Eisenhower became president of Columbia University. A great convocation was set up to greet the famous general in his new role at this large university. Thousands of students were present. Ike walked onto the platform, looked down at the students who apparently impressed him as being super-serious and expecting a moralistic talk urging them to study hard. Instead, with the famous Eisenhower grin, he said, "Have fun! I mean it. The day that goes by without your having had some fun—the day you don't enjoy life—is not only unnecessary but unchristian!"[1]

You say that sounds good for kids, but what about us adults? There is no question about it, raising a family is physically and emotionally exhausting. There are so many things to do: earning a living; making a dollar stretch; making decisions; solving problems; administering discipline; washing and cooking; and a van full of other duties. As you parents know all too well, today you really have to be on your toes all the time. But it is most important that you take the time to relax and enjoy living together as a family.

There is nothing more important or more Christian than for you to be fun to live with. Hear these timely words from the ancient Scriptures: "What does one really get from hard work? I have thought about this in connection with all the various kinds of work God has given to mankind. Everything is appropriate in its own time. But though God has planted

1. Dr. Norman Vincent Peale, *Foundation for Christian Living.* Pauling, New York. June, 1975 issue. Used by permission.

eternity in the hearts of men, even so, man cannot see the whole scope of God's work from beginning to end. So I conclude that, first, there is nothing better for a man than to be happy and to enjoy himself as long as he can; and second, that he should eat and drink and enjoy the fruits of his labors, for these are gifts from God" (Ecclesiastes 3:9-13).

1. *Get high on Jesus.* There is tremendous joy in personally knowing Jesus Christ and living his abundant life-style. Jesus said, "I am come that [you] might have life, and that [you] might have it more abundantly" (John 10:10, KJV). The Lord Jesus wants you to enjoy yourself as you make your journey through this life. He wants to eliminate the negative from your life and activate the positive.

Dr. Norman Vincent Peale tells about being in a joyful gathering of alive Christians where these glowing testimonies were given:

> A beautiful lady got up and said, "I want to witness to the joy that is in my life. I am an alcoholic like some others here, but I have been dry for three years through the power of the Lord. Christian friends actually found me down in the gutter in the midst of booze and immorality. They picked me up, loved me with Christian love and stayed with me." Someone remarked, "You certainly

don't look like a down-and-outer now, what happened?" The lady simply gave this moving reply, "Jesus did it. Jesus made the difference with me."

Then a couple stood up and told about constant fighting and how they had been unfaithful to one another. They had come to the point where they hated each other's guts. "But," they said, "we are together now, and we are falling in love all over again." Those present could see that it was true because of the way they put their arms around each other and looked into each other's eyes. What a beautiful reconciliation. And then someone asked, "How did this change happen?" "Jesus did it!" they declared.[2]

Jesus is the joy of living, he is the dearest friend to me. In the days of my growing up, there was a little chorus we sang many times:

If you want joy, real joy,
    wonderful joy,
Let Jesus come into your heart,
Your sins He'll take away,
Your night He'll turn to day,
Your life, He'll make it over anew.

2. Adapted from *Foundation for Christian Living* by Norman Vincent Peale, June 1975 issue. Used by permission.

If you want joy, real joy,
    wonderful joy,
Let Jesus come into your life.

Get high on Jesus and be more fun to live
with.

   2. *Laugh your way into fun and rich
fellowship with your family members.* An
ingredient urgently needed in every person's
life can be learned from watching a little
baby. Our blond-headed, blue-eyed baby Ann
has it. I love to watch her crawl all over our
house from one room to the other. She enjoys
every minute of her high adventure. Along
the trail she'll pause from time to time, pick
up a toy, stick it in her mouth, drop it, and give
a funny little laugh. Whenever I get down on
the floor with her and play the game,
"Where's Annie," she soon breaks out with
uninhibited laughter. Before I know it she has
me rolling in laughter. Hearty laughter is
great fun for every age.

   Howard G. Hendricks, in his book *Heaven
Help the Home,* illustrates the importance of
intervals of pleasure and enjoyment, with this
true story:

   We have had two graduates at Dallas
   Seminary from the same home. If I had to
   pick two men from our alumni who are
   making an impact for the Saviour, I
   would choose these products of a humble

peach-farm home in California. I stayed in that home some time ago, and came away saying, "O God, reproduce this all over America."

Once I asked one of these boys, "Hey, Ed, what do you remember most about your father?" He pondered my question for a moment.

"Two things—and interestingly enough, they appear to be contradictory. I used to throw a paper route, and I had to get up at four A.M. I'd go by my father's room and the door would be cracked, and I'd see him on his knees in prayer. That made a profound impression on me. The second thing I remember is my father rolling on the floor with us kids in laughter." What an invincible combination! On his knees in prayer and on the floor with laughter! By the way, what will they remember you for?[3]

Do those you live with a big favor. Get into the habit of laughing. Back in my teen years I spent each summer working on the grounds of a church camp across the street from where we lived. It was my privilege to get to know some pretty marvelous Christians. One man I'll never forget is Ernest Eades, who was a

3. Howard G. Hendricks, *Heaven Help the Home* (Wheaton, Illinois: Victor Books, 1973), p. 97. Used by permission.

missionary in the Cape Verdes Islands. Having had some sudden changes in his scheduling of church visitation, he spent six weeks working with six of us teenagers on the grounds of the camp. This Britisher had a delightful sense of humor. The more we teased him about his "spot of tea" every morning at ten o'clock, the more he joked and teased us, and we all had a grand time together. That was one of the best summers ever.

One day I asked this veteran missionary why he was always so jovial and fun to be with. He confessed that it hadn't always been that way. When he first went to the field as a missionary, he was far too serious-minded, and it had begun to tell the story on his nervous system which was being wound up tighter and tighter. Then the Lord Jesus showed him how good humor and healthy laughter could release tension and make life fun to live. In Ecclesiastes 3:4 we read: "A time to laugh..." When life gets too serious, when you are taking yourself too seriously, or are becoming too serious about other people, the time has come for you to put your head back and let the laughter flow.

3. *Plan and participate in family recreation.* Everyone needs to spend some time at play. Our Lord said to his tired disciples, "Come ye yourselves apart ... and rest a while" (Mark 6:31, KJV). Someone has said that if you don't come apart, you'll come apart. Not only does

all work and no play make you dull, but it can make you come apart at the seams. When the pressures of everyday life begin to get to you, and you feel those tensions building up, that's when you need to relieve your emotions with recreation.

To add zip to your body, zest to your spirit, and fun to your living, take the time to relax and play.

Recreation brings family members closer together. My father was a very busy and active man, carrying heavy and serious responsibilities. Without compromise, dad annually set aside the last three weeks in August for our family vacation in the scenic outdoors of Ontario, Canada. Once we arrived at Frog Rapids Fishing Camp, located on the point where endless blue lakes come together, my dad became the man he was. The administrative responsibilities of overseeing 135 churches in central Ohio dropped off his shoulders and he became the adventuring outdoorsman. There was nothing he loved more than to roam the lakes in the family boat. Fishing, boating, picnicking, sitting around an open fire, picking blueberries, and just having fun together are priceless treasures in my boyhood memories. It wasn't what we did so much; it was just the fact that we were together. It was through these play times that we drew together and built deep and lasting relationships as a family. The family who plays together not only stays together, but family members learn to relate one to another.

A couple whom I liked a lot wanted me to help them have a happier marriage. They had a problem of not being able to communicate one with the other. When we were together in my office at a counseling session they would talk and they would listen, but once they left there wouldn't be much communication of any depth until they came back for another appointment.

One day I hit on the idea of what to do to help them. It sounded a little silly, but I got them to promise to do it anyway. Here was the big therapy that I gave them to do every night: take a fifteen-minute walk together; do it every night whether you say anything to each other or not. It seemed simple enough. They promised to do it, and they did it.

When they came back a couple of weeks later, the most miraculous change had taken place. Their communication had come alive and they were enjoying each other so much more. As they had walked together each evening, relaxed, and just enjoying the outdoors and being with each other, they started talking and listening to one another, sharing with each other and enjoying being together. Yes, doing things together can put renewed joy into your family life.

Family recreation is something you have to plan. Fail to plan, and you plan to fail.

Everything else that happens in your life happens because you plan it. The simple fact is that if you don't plan activities, set the time, and put the date on the calendar, the days will go by, the weeks will pass, and you'll look back and wonder how the most important things in your life got left out.

Family recreation is something that you must do now. Don't be like the foolish farmer who was so preoccupied in his business that he kept building and expanding without stopping to enjoy the good things in everyday life. He was trying to store up more and more riches, just one more barn to build and then he'd take some time off. Jesus said that the man was a fool because he died without ever building a relationship with God.

It doesn't take much imagination to see a man who never took the time to enjoy recreation with his family members. By the time he stopped, it was too late. As James says, "For what is your life? It is even a vapour, that appeareth for a little time, and then vanisheth away" (James 4:14, KJV). It will never be more convenient than now to plan your family recreation.

Fun-packed suggestions for happy family recreation:

1. Have a little fun every day. Carve out a few minutes each day to get down on the floor and play with small children in the home. If you have the privilege of having teenagers in

your home, take just a few minutes each day to enter into their world and enjoy with them what they are interested in. It is not the amount of time spent, but the quality of time that pays rich dividends.

2. Take a day off and spend it together as a family. How about doing something the children want to do?

3. Designate one night a week as family night. This may be a night when everyone is at home together for recreation and activity, or it may mean going somewhere together. At times it could mean father doing something with the boys while mother does something with the girls—or the reverse. Intentionally reserve one night of the week for each other.

4. Enjoy a family vacation together. For a real close experience on a low budget, try camping out together.

5. Cultivate and encourage creativeness. You don't have to spend lots of money to have fun. Some of the most fun things cost little or nothing. Use your imagination. Things we make ourselves or make up are always more fun anyway. The cards I cherish most are those that my family members have created especially for me.

6. Make it a family project to write down the many recreational activities that you might do as a family. You may want to divide into sections those things which cost little and those things which are more expensive.

7. Enrich your family life by having other Christian families in for a time of inter-family activity and recreation.

8. Make birthdays and special days big family celebrations. By doing this, you will add anticipation, excitement, and spontaneous joy to your family life.

9. Participation is the key to success. Allow each family member, from the youngest to the oldest, to be involved in the selection of family recreation. For the most fun for everyone, make it a truly sharing experience from beginning to end.

4. *Love the little things in life and they will love you back.* A group of boys and girls were asked to list the things that made them happiest. The answers are rather revealing. Here are some of the things the boys enjoyed: flying a kite, looking into a deep ravine, carving on a stick, building a fort in the sand, running after a rabbit. Here is what some of the girls said made them happy: baking cookies, dressing up in mother's old clothes, watching the moon in the sky. Yes, little children know how to love the little things and that's one of the reasons they are so much fun to be with.

In the summer of 1973 it was our privilege at New Hope Community Church to have as our special guest Miss Terry Ann Meeuwsen, that year's Miss America. Not only did our people enjoy hearing her sing so magnificently, but they fell in love with her as

a beautiful person. Terry radiated the
abundant life Jesus had given to her. All of
our staff who had the opportunity of getting
to know her in a more personal way felt her
excitement and joy about life. After she had
given her witness for Christ and the service
had ended, multitudes of people pushed to
the front to shake her hand, and in many
instances, to get an autograph.

Amidst all this attention from a large
crowd, I saw Terry stop and direct all of her
attention to a little girl whose ribbon had
come undone in her hair. With a big smile, and
really enjoying herself, Terry tied the little
girl's ribbon. We had so much fun having
Terry with us for a day that when she left we
felt we had been friends for a long time. The
most fun people I have ever known are those
who pay attention to and enjoy the little
things.

Jesus loved the birds, the lilies, the crops,
and the children at play. He was glad to be
alive. He loved the little things and they
loved him back, and he was so much fun to be
with. Open your eyes to the little things; love
them, and they'll love you back. And you will
be so much more fun to be with.

5. *To be fun to live with, just keep on
praising the Lord.* The tremendous secret
of enjoying life, of having a positive
mental attitude, is to do what it says in
1 Thessalonians 5:18: "In every thing give

thanks, for this is the will of God in Christ Jesus concerning you" (KJV). The more you praise the Lord, the more fun you will be.

When we praise the Lord, these tremendous things happen to us:

Release comes from tensions and anxieties.
We become aware that God is good and
     that he is in control.
Our minds focus on the positive.
Spiritual power and victory flow into our
     inner spirit.
There is peace in the midst of outer storm.
Our entire being gets in step with the plan
     and purposes of God.
With greater expectation we have the
     living hope that the best is yet to come.
So let's do what Bill Gaither's song says:

Let's just praise the Lord,
Praise the Lord,
Let's just lift our hands toward heaven,
and praise the Lord.[4]

---

4. "Let's Just Praise the Lord," used by permission. © 1972 by William J. Gaither.

CHAPTER SIX
Build Self-esteem in Those You Love

Although John Chustz lived with his family just a few blocks from us in a quiet, almost country neighborhood, I had never heard of him until I saw his picture on the front page of our morning newspaper. Bold headlines announced a shocking massacre: "WEST LINN TEENAGER SHOOTS HIS PARENTS, BROTHER, HIMSELF." Why would a nineteen-year-old, with all his future ahead of him, premeditate and commit such a hideous crime? If a person were to do a thorough investigation of what set off the fuse of murder inside of this young man, one would no doubt discover that John was off the beam because of extremely low self-esteem. What untold misery is suffered by and inflicted upon families because of low self-esteem.

95

A vast number of American women are suffering from low self-esteem. In the past twelve years of pastoral counseling with women of all ages, I have repeatedly heard the devastating feeling of worthlessness expressed in a variety of ways. A questionnaire, recently administered to a cross-section of women for the purpose of determining the causes of depression, revealed that, more than anything else, low self-esteem caused feelings of depression.

Ladies, allow me to let you in on a little secret. You are not the only ones suffering from low self-esteem. In our competitive world many a man painfully knows what it is to struggle with inferiority feelings. Believe it or not, the lack of self-confidence resulting from low self-esteem is an overwhelming problem among teenagers. The teenager who is convinced that he is not worth much, is the most susceptible to drugs, illicit sex, and other kinds of irresponsible behavior.

I think it would be conservative to estimate that 90 percent of the people alive in our world today are crippled and hindered by varying degrees of inadequate feelings about themselves. An individual who is beaten down by low self-esteem finds it so much more difficult to get along in family relationships. If one is not happy with himself, how can he be happy with those he lives with every day? Chances are that members of your own household presently suffer from low self-esteem and need your help. Family members who enjoy good, healthy feelings about themselves are freed from the need to center on their miserable selves and find it so much easier to give love. The way to make your home a happier, more loving place, is for you to do what you can to build self-esteem in those you love.

Happy family-building question: How do you build self-esteem in those you love?

BUILD YOUR LOVED ONES' SELF-ESTEEM BY BUILDING THEIR FAITH IN GOD.

I firmly believe that the most valuable contribution any parent can make to his child is to instill in him a genuine faith in God. There is no greater feeling of worth than to know the Creator of this vast universe "loves me personally." With your loved ones sing it out and experience this little, yet mighty song, "Yes, Jesus Loves Me: The Bible Tells Me So."

Teach each of your loved ones that God values him more than all the possessions in this entire world. God the Father understands us. He knows all our fears and anxieties, our aspirations and dreams. In his immeasurable love, he steadfastly reaches out to us. When everyone else stops caring, he still cares. God sent Jesus Christ, his Son, to die for everything that is wrong with us, because he loves us. The fact is that if you were the only person who had ever lived, Jesus would have died just for you. In this generous outpouring of love God is saying, "You are worth saving."

One of a kind, that's you. God made you unique—you are a divine original. You don't have to be as good as, or like, someone else. God never intended for you to be anyone but yourself. What God asks of you is that you develop into the beautiful person he made you to be. Bill Gaither, the current popular gospel song writer, expresses this uniqueness of each individual in the little children's song that he wrote for his little daughter. Fill your loved one's mind with these words from "Something Special":[1]

> That's why he made you special:
> You're the only one of your kind.
> God gave you a body,
> A bright, healthy mind.
> He had a special purpose
> That he wanted you to find,
> So he made you something special:
> You're the only one of your kind.

1. "You're Something Special," © 1974, by William J. Gaither, used by permission.

"Worth loving" includes everyone in your family. To make your home a happier place, help your loved ones to discover:

The plan and purpose God has for their
  lives;
The talents God has placed within them and
  how those talents can be developed;
The unlimited potential for good that God
  has given to them;
The inner quality of beauty that is
  distinctly theirs to express and expand.

My dad and mother started me on the pathway to healthy self-esteem when they planted within me a strong faith in God. In our home on the outskirts of Columbus, Ohio, God was real and alive, present every day, and as a result, our family relationships were healthy and happy.

In this kind of Christian home atmosphere family members can help each other to develop the healthy self-concept which Christ taught. The individual is neither haughty nor worthless, but just right—having a humble reverence for God and every member of the human race, seeing others as neither better nor worse than himself, but with Christ's help learning to love others as himself.

Only where God is given his rightful place as heavenly Father do children grow up experiencing the feeling of worth and dignity that God created them to enjoy.

HERE ARE EIGHT THINGS YOU CAN DO TO MAKE YOUR LOVED ONES FEEL THAT THEY ARE PERSONS OF TREMENDOUS WORTH AND VALUE:

1. *Show your loved ones they are worthwhile persons by the manner in which you honor and respect them.* I was sitting in my parked car in a middle-class neighborhood waiting for a friend, when I heard a man berating his son. Apparently the boy had been assigned to do some yard work, but what he had done somehow didn't suit his father. So this irate man yelled at his own boy, "You stupid little jerk, can't you ever do anything right?" Profanity and insults one after another, like hurled rocks, struck the defenseless little boy. Is this the way you want to treat your loved ones?

A friend of mine who is a real go-getter and is the epitome of business success, confided in me that when it came to being a handyman around his house, he was a complete failure. The reason he avoided getting involved in any handyman work around his house was because he didn't think he was capable. His past experience was that when he had attempted to do this sort of work he really got uptight. Analyzing this, my good friend discovered that the reason for his lack of self-confidence in his ability as a handyman grew out of his boyhood. Any time he tried to do any work, it was never good enough to please his father. His father always put him down as being a poor handyman. How tragic it is to destroy self-esteem in someone you love.

How appreciative I am that my father and mother taught my brother and me respect and honor by the respectful manner in which they alway talked to us as human beings. They always made us feel like somebody, instead of nobody. It is a lasting tribute to my Christian father that I can never remember hearing him speak about anyone or to another human being in a disrespectful fashion. Here is the payoff—as a result of my dad's spiritual example in our home, it has always been very easy for me to keep the commandment, "Honor your father and mother" (Ephesians 6:2).

Honor and respect is not only taught but caught when a husband and wife practice this knitting-together verse: "So again I say, a man must love his wife as a part of himself; and the wife must see to it that she deeply respects her husband—obeying, praising and honoring him" (Ephesians 5:33).

2. *Become sensitive to and protective of your loved ones' feelings.* Everyone has feelings, just like you do, from the youngest member of the family to the oldest. Is there anything more fragile than the human spirit? What a wonderful thing it would be if every family

member would put a sign on each loved one, reading: "Handle with care by being considerate of all my feelings." The Bible calls us to kindness with these words, "In response to all he has done for us, let us outdo each other in being helpful and kind to each other and in doing good" (Hebrews 10:24).

When the spirit of a wife is wounded, however unintentionally, her self-esteem suffers and the very spirit of the marriage is damaged. In order to make us more aware of this important area, here are some recurring ways in which a man can bruise and wound the spirit of his wife: by having his priorities confused and giving her the feeling she isn't first place in his life; by being inconsiderate in not being punctual for dinner; by failing to recognize and openly express appreciation of her attempts to please him; making unfavorable comparisons of her with other women; by his own lack of spiritual leadership; by failing to show interest in what she is doing; by not placing value on her opinions, or failing to ask for them; by taking her for granted, instead of continuing to be thankful that God made her his.

Men, let us heed these words of the Lord: "You husbands must be careful of your wives, being thoughtful of their needs, honoring them as the weaker sex. Remember that you and your wife are partners in receiving God's blessings, and if you don't treat her as you should, your prayers will not get ready answers" (1 Peter 3:7).

Wives, stop wounding the spirit of your husbands. Every time you wound the spirit of your husband, the gauge on his self-esteem drops another notch and the very spirit of your relationship is damaged. Here are some ways wives wound the spirit of their husbands: (1) By making something else first place. I've seen mothers self-righteously proud of the fact that they are putting their children first—and by so doing, drive their husbands away from the marriage bed to the waiting arms of another woman. (2) Your husband can be deeply hurt when you don't recognize his attempt to please you, or when you neglect to express gratitude for the kind gesture he has shown. (3) Comparing your man to another "more successful" man may break his heart. A man is deeply wounded when a woman belittles or rejects his ideas. (4) Lack of responsiveness to his sexual advances can wound his male ego. It is your responsiveness that can make him feel like superman. (5) Undercutting his discipline of the children can wound his spirit. (6) Rebelling against his leadership in public can put him down very low. (7) Being uninterested in his work can cause him to stop communicating. (8) Not recognizing his talents and encouraging him to develop them can make him crawl into a shell and make him stay. If you have been guilty of any of these or of wounding your man's spirit in any other way, the time to stop is now.

On one of the first sunny days of spring my wife, Margi, asked me at the breakfast table if she might take me to work and have the car to do some shopping. Bubbling with springtime enthusiasm, she told me about the plants she was going to purchase for our yard, and then added that she was going to buy me a surprise. Having my mind fixed on our need to save money in the next couple of weeks I let her know in no uncertain terms that I expected her to live within her allotted allowance. Now this was really a dumb thing for me to say, because she had been doing exceptionally well in managing the portion of the family budget that was hers to look after. My remarks were completely uncalled for and, worse yet, they were unfair. I had wounded her spirit and had succeeded only in killing her joy.

A few hours later in my office, as I thought about this, I became aware of what I had done. I called Margi on the phone, telling her I was sorry, that I had been out of line and that I wanted her to forgive me for wounding her spirit. She did and the spirit of oneness in our relationship was restored.

No matter how sensitive we become to our mate's feelings, from time to time we are going to wound the spirit of our beloved. Recognize it when you do. Immediately confess your failure and ask for forgiveness, and the spirit of your marriage will be renewed again and again and will grow and bloom in beauty.

Needed: parental sensitivity to children's feelings. Too often I have heard parents describe their little monster, sparing none of the colorful, gory details, right in front of guess who—their child. How degrading; how destructive of self-esteem.

To build self-esteem in your child start breaking the will and stop breaking the spirit. Dr. James Dobson, in his compelling approach for parents and teachers, *Hide or Seek,* had this to say, "It is very important to understand the difference between breaking the *spirit* of a child, and breaking his *will*. The human spirit is exceedingly fragile at all ages and must be handled with care. It involves a person's view of himself, his personal worth and the emotional factors to which this book is dedicated. A parent can damage his child's spirit very easily—by ridicule, disrespect, threats to withdraw love, and verbal rejection. Anything that depreciates his self-esteem is costly to his spirit. However, while the spirit is brittle and must be treated gently, the will is made of steel. It is full strength at the moment of birth, as any midnight bottle-warmer knows. Even a child whose spirit has been crushed can present the most awesome display of wilful power. We want, then, to shape the will of a child, but leave his spirit intact."[2]

3. *Be responsive to your loved one.* What is the opposite of the word response? No answer; no response; completely ignoring what the other person has said or done. When you are on the receiving end of this kind of treatment, how does it make you feel? I'll tell you how it makes me feel: it makes me feel like I'm not worth the person's effort to respond. Somerset Maugham said, "The tragedy of love is not death or separating, the tragedy of love is indifference."

Some years ago I had an acquaintance with whom I had to spend a lot of time, and because we were together a lot, I made several attempts to share something of myself with him. Consistently he would ignore what I said and with no further ado start into one of his endless monologues. He never made me feel good about myself as a person and after awhile I found myself feeling bad about him and trying to avoid his company.

I now have a very enjoyable friend by the name of Jerry. It seems that no matter what I want to talk about or to share with him, he is not only an attentive listener, but he has a way of interacting with me that I greatly enjoy. He makes me feel that I am an important person, and I think he is one of the

2. James Dobson, *Hide or Seek* (Old Tappan, New Jersey: Fleming H. Revell Company, 1974), p. 85. Used by permission.

most marvelous persons I've ever known. What is the difference between these two people? The first man, by being unresponsive to what I said, threw cold water on my self-esteem; my good friend, Jerry, by responding with interaction, always builds my self-esteem.

There is nothing that makes us feel more important and worthwhile than for a loved one to really listen to us and interact in a way that says, "What you have said is important." I know it makes me feel good when my wife thinks that I'm important enough to listen to and interact with. You can do it—you can help build self-esteem in your loved ones by concentrating on being responsive to what they communicate.

Approximately an hour after the evening meal, little Brian taps on daddy's newspaper and says, "Look what I've drawn!" Not even looking up from the newspaper, daddy barks, "Beat it, kid!" Dejected, Brian looks all through the house until he finally tracks down mother who is ironing clothes in the back bedroom. Once again he straightens up with a bright smile. "Look what I've drawn," he says as he holds up his prize. Mother glances downward for a brief moment and says, "Uh-huh." Obviously she is absorbed in her own little world and has not really heard Brian. I ask you—how important does little Brian feel at this moment? Opportunity to build Brian's self-esteem has forever been lost.

Christian love can never be passive; it must always be active. To love Christ's way, I must be ever ready to be actively concerned with the loved person. Love is responsive to the other person—what greater place to love responsively than in our family relationships?

We build self-esteem in our mate when we respond to him or her sexually. This is one reason why the Bible urges us to respond to our marriage partner wholeheartedly. "The man should give his wife all that is her right as a married woman, and the wife should do the same for her husband: for a girl who marries no longer has full right to her own body, for her husband then has his rights to it, too; and in the same way the husband no longer has full right to his own body, for it belongs to his wife. So do not refuse these rights to each other" (1 Corinthians 7:3-5).

4. *Build self-esteem in your loved ones by giving each his own responsibilities.* Persons grow and are made to feel important if they are given, and accept responsibilities. There is a direct relationship between self-esteem and responsibilities. Nobody ever feels very worthwhile who doesn't have a responsible job. It is through becoming responsible for oneself and for other people that new heights of self-esteem are reached. A three-year-old child needs to have appropriate

responsibilities assigned to him to fit his age. These assignments need to be taught not only by telling, but also by showing. Husband and wife can each build self-esteem in the other by mutually agreeing on responsibilities worthy of each one's attention and management. Let your loved ones know that you love them enough to demand that they behave as responsible persons.

5. *Highlight and encourage interest areas.* You can help your loved one to counterbalance his feelings of inferiority and weaknesses by capitalizing on his strengths. Everyone needs to excel in at least one thing in order to feel good about himself. It is absolutely amazing what being an expert or champion in just one thing can do to put self-confidence into one's entire personality.

I wholeheartedly agree with Dr. Dobson when he says, "I recommend that you, [the child's] parent, make a careful assessment of his area of strength. Then select a skill where you believe the greatest possibilities for success lie. Once this selection is made, see that he gets through the first stage. Reward him, push him, threaten him, beg him—bribe him if necessary but make him learn it. If you discover later that you have made a mistake, back up and start over on something else."[3] Take the time, put forth the effort to help your

3. Dobson, *Hide or Seek,* p. 73.

child develop his or her own special area of interest. You're on the beam when you build self-esteem in those you love.

6. *Build self-esteem in those you love by being honest and open about your own shortcomings.* I have noticed that people who do not admit their shortcomings or confess their faults to one another are plagued with low self-esteem. Why is this? The answer is that perfectionism is an impossible standard. No matter how one tries to masquerade and pretend that he is without flaw, deep inside he knows he does not measure up to the standard; thus feelings of low self-esteem are nurtured. Children learn from their parents, and one of the best things you can do as a parent is openly, at home, practice this verse, "Admit your faults to one another and pray for each other so that you may be healed" (James 5:16). When you do this, you are teaching your children to be honest and open in their relationships, and that one does not have to perform perfectly to be worthwhile. A worthwhile person is not a perfect person but a confessing, growing person.

I am a Christian today because of what Jesus Christ has done for me. He has, by the gift of his grace, given me the wonderful name, Christian. Now, with his help, I am daily growing into that name. "An evil man is stubborn, but a godly man will reconsider" (Proverbs 21:29). You build self-esteem in those you love every time you use any of these words: I am sorry. You were right, I was wrong. I'm not sure about this ... what do you think we ought to do?

7. *Let your loved one know that in your eyes he is a beautiful person.* One does not have to be physically attractive to be a truly beautiful person. You can help your loved ones to grow in beauty from the inside out by consistently expressing appreciation for their finer qualities. "Don't be conceited about the outward beauty that depends on jewelry, or beautiful clothes, or hair arrangement. Be beautiful inside, in your hearts, with the lasting charm of a gentle and quiet spirit which is so precious to God. That kind of deep beauty was seen in the saintly women of old, who trusted God and fitted in with their husbands' plans" (1 Peter 3:3-5). Appreciate the deeper values in your loved one, and follow the advice of Proverbs: "Praise her for the many fine things she does" (Proverbs 31:31).

The Bible study group that my wife, Margi, leads each week has witnessed some fantastic results in improved family relationships due to the participants applying biblical principles. A few weeks ago, one of the gals shared how the Lord showed her that she was damaging her ten-year-old son by nagging at him all the time instead of building him up as a person of worth and value.

Vince is a nice, likeable kid, just as cute as

can be. His mother, Judy, told how she watched outside her window when it was time for Vince to come home from school. Here he came down the street, happy, singing, skipping along, but just as he came to the corner to make the last turn, a few hundred feet from the front door of his home, his manner abruptly changed. He stopped skipping and singing, dropped his head and shoulders, and started shuffling his feet along like he was a ninety-year-old man. Vince was dreading walking in the front door and getting nit-picked at by his mother. Judy, with an aching heart, watched for several days as she saw the same scene repeated over and over.

With a heavy heart this mother asked Jesus to help her change this unacceptable picture, to stop destroying her son's self-esteem and to start building it. With this new insight, she greeted Vince at the door with a big smile and a warm, "Hello, Vince. How was your day today?"

She started telling him, "You are a neat kid, Vince." She started picking out his good points and bragging about him. Instead of continuing to crab at him for going into the kitchen and making a mess, she began preparing his snack for him and had it waiting when he came home, showing him that he was an important person.

With tears of joy, this beaming mother shared with her friends her one-hundred-eighty-degree change from destroying

her son's self-esteem to building it
up. One week after this growing Christian
mother changed, when it was time for Vince
to come home from school she looked out the
window. Here he came, running, skipping,
jumping, singing, all the way home. Up the
front stairs Vince ran, opened the door, and
yelled, "Hello, Mom!"

Home is a great place to be when your
mother builds your self-esteem. "So encourage
each other to build each other up"
(1 Thessalonians 5:11).

8. *Build self-esteem in those you love by
letting them know you believe in them.* Bob
Richards, the well-known pole vaulter, tells
the story about a great baseball player. Carl
Erskine was pitching in the World Series for
his team in Brooklyn, which was ahead two
games to one and was leading the third game
5 to 2. The hitter came up to the plate and Carl
walked him. Another fellow came up and Carl
walked him. Then big Johnny Mize stepped up
with two men on base. Carl pitched one in the
wrong spot and Johnny boomed the ball into
the outfield seats. The score was tied.

At that moment Carl felt he had blown the
game, let his teammates down. Coach
Charlie Dressen came off the bench and said,
"Carl, how do you feel?" He said, "I'm all right."
But actually, he felt rotten. Then the coach
took him by the arm and said, "Carl, you are
my man. I'm leaving you in. I believe in you.

You can do it." Carl later said, "It's hard to describe what it did for me to know that my coach believed in me, to know that my teammates were behind me. That belief alone gave me the courage to put forth my best effort. He retired the next sixteen men in order. Three days later the Dodgers won the Series behind his brilliant pitching.[4]

Believe in another person and that person will live up to your belief. Years ago, before going to assume the pastorate of one of my first churches, the church official told me that a particular man in the congregation was a hopeless pervert. He said, "Stay away from him. Don't have anything to do with him. He is beyond help." You know what I did? I went to that church, I put my arm around that man, I went over to his house, I had dinner with him and his family, I let him know that I loved him in Christian love and that I believed in him. During the time I pastored that church that man would do anything I asked him to do. If it was mowing the yard, whatever it was, he would be there and he would do it. And the most amazing thing happened. Because someone believed in him, he became a clean and righteous man.

What a lift it is to have a loved one believe in you!

4. J. Allan Petersen, ed., *For Men Only* (Wheaton, Illinois: Tyndale House Publishers, 1974), pp. 204, 205. Used by permission.

Scores of people can be changed for the better if someone will touch them on the shoulder and say, "I believe in you." This touch of faith can make all the difference. A marvelous Christian lady in our church recently related that when she was a teenager growing up, she knew her parents believed in her and trusted her. She said that when she went out on dates, this trust caused her to keep herself clean and living according to Christian values. There are a lot of teenagers who need a touch on the shoulder by their father or their mother saying, "I believe in you. I know you are going through some rough waters, but we have the faith that you will come out on top."

There are some husbands who find themselves without a job. There is nothing more difficult for a man than to be unable to provide for his family. Desperately, the man with the wounded ego needs his wife to take his hand and say, "I understand. I believe in you. It's going to work out O.K." The wife, at this time in their lives, needs a husband to put his arms around her and say, "I love you. I know this is a difficult time for you, but I believe you are going to come through it with flying colors."

I am indeed a fortunate person; the two outstanding women in my life believe in me. My mother, now past seventy years of age, has always believed in me. No matter what I've done, where I've been, or what has happened, she always believes the best in me. I can count on her; she is on my side, determined that I am going to be God's man. Into my life God has brought my wife, Margi. When I met her I was at the lowest ebb of my life. I had been broken apart by a shattering experience, yet she saw beyond my confusion and brokenness and through eyes of love, believed in me. No matter what mistakes I make, I know she believes in me. How thankful I am to God for these loved ones who show me his love in action in its purest, most uplifting way.

A happy family is where imperfect persons are committed in love to other imperfect persons, where each becomes an open channel of God's love to help the other grow and bloom in the beauty of love. What a difference it makes when someone believes in you: intentionally, consistently, conscientiously, fervently, faithfully.

Build self-esteem in those closest to you and all of a sudden, in some moment of time, you will realize that all the while you have been building your own self-esteem. Jesus promised, "Give and it shall be given unto you" (Luke 6:38, KJV).

Date Due

Code 4386-04, CLS-4, Broadman Supplies, Nashville, Tenn.,
Printed in U.S.A.